MAKE ME LAUGH!

GRIN AND BEAR IT

ZOO JOKES TO MAKE YOU ROAR

by Sharon Friedman and Irene Shere with
Diane L. Burns, John Jansen, and Thomas Mase
pictures by Brian Gable

Carolrhoda Books, Inc. • Minneapolis

Q: If you spotted a large reptile in a passageway between buildings, what would it probably be?

A: An alley-gator.

Q: What do possums eat as they hang from trees?

A: Upside-down cake.

Q: What is a camel's favorite snack food?

A: Camel-corn.

Q: If a monkey is like his father, what is he often called?

A: A chimp off the old block.

Q: What does a bear say on a cold winter night?

A: Bearrrr (brrrr).

Q: What does a bear do on a bad day?

A: Grin and bear it.

Q: What goes clomp, clomp, clomp, swish, clomp, clomp, clomp, swish?

A: An elephant with one wet sneaker.

Q: Why did the elephant wear green sneakers?

A: Because his blue ones were wet.

Q: What's a bear's favorite nursery rhyme?

A: "Here We Go Round the Mul-bear-ry Bush."

Q: Why did the elephant change her socks on the golf course?

A: She got a hole in one.

Q: Have crocodiles learned to cook in microwave ovens?

A: No. They're still using croc pots.

Q: What mammal is born extremely immature, stays in its mother's pouch for months, eats fruit and flowers, and is real cool?

A: An opossum on vacation at the North Pole.

Q: What is the favorite food of the South American llama?

A: Llama beans.

Q: How did the bear get through this book?

A: Just bear-ly.

Q: How did the cowboy elephant burn himself?

A: Trying to make himself at home on the range.

Q: Why did the kangaroo like to play pool?

A: The ball always went into her pocket.

Q: What did the bear call the story of her life?

A: Her auto-bear-ography.

Q: What did the dolphin say when his trainer accused him of ruining the show?

A: "I didn't do it on porpoise."

Q: What marsupial eats grass and stings?

A: A walla-bee.

Q: Which sea lion has a permanent home in the White House?

A: The presidential seal.

Q: What do bears take for a bad headache?

A: As-bear-in (aspirin).

Q: What do you get when you cross a wallaby with a clock?

A: A pocket watch.

Q: Why was the elephant's face blue?

A: His tennis shoes were tied too tight.

Q: What do you call a bat that wears a big wool sweater?

A: A wombat.

Q: What does a bear do during the winter months?

A: Hi-bear-nate.

Q: Why don't elephants do well in karate class?

A: Even when their belts aren't too tight, they can't kick very high.

Q: What kind of dog rescued the bear when he was stranded in the Alps?

A: A St. Bear-nard.

Q: Why are wombats always in debt?

A: Because they are burrowers.

Q: What's the hardest thing for a stampeding elephant to catch?

A: Her breath.

Q: What meal does a bear eat when he sleeps through breakfast?

A: Bear-runch (brunch).

Q: Do elephant tourists like to go swimming?

A: Yes, when they remember to pack their trunks.

Q: How do elephant basketball teams score points?

A: They slam-trunk the ball.

Q: What famous British bear wrote Romeo and Juliet?

A: William Shakes-bear.

Q: Where was the smoke coming from on the bear's car?

A: The car-bear-ator.

Q: How does an elephant make a strawberry shake?

A: She takes it to a scary movie.

Q: What kind of elephant can you find in a box of popcorn?

A: A very small one.

Q: How did the kangaroo exercise?

A: She did her jumping jacks.

Q: Why did the elephant take a raisin to the movies?

A: He couldn't find a date.

Q: Where do bears go to get books?

A: The li-bear-y.

Q: Why are kangaroos such good workers?
A: They always hop to it.

Q: What roadblock stopped visitors from entering the bear army camp?
A: A bear-ricade.

Q: What's a bear's favorite dinosaur?
A: Bear-ontosaurus.

Q: Why did the elephant eat bullets?
A: She wanted to grow bangs.

Q: What's a bear's favorite fruit?
A: Straw-bear-ries.

Q: Was the kangaroo nervous?
A: No, she was just a little jumpy.

Q: What screeched when the bear's car came to a stop?
A: Bear-akes.

Q: What do you get when you cross an ostrich with a blue-winged duck?

A: A really big teal.

Q: What do marsupials have that no other animal can have?

A: Baby marsupials.

Q: What did Mr. and Mrs. Bear take on their camping trip?

A: The bear necessities.

Q: What marsupial grows the fastest?

A: The kangaroo. It grows by leaps and bounds.

Q: How does one bear say good-bye to another bear?

A: With a bear hug.

Q: When the gorilla got a pain in her stomach, what did the doctors call it?

A: Ape-pendicitis.

Q: Can you name eight marsupials?

A: A wombat, an opossum, a koala, a wallaby, a bandicoot, and three kangaroos.

Q: Where do most condors make their nests?

A: In condor-miniums.

Q: What is a buffalo's favorite dessert?

A: Bison-berry pie.

Q: What do you call the first elephant in the bathtub?

A: The ringleader.

Q: What did the scientist say when she discovered a wildcat thought to be extinct?

A: "I've found the missing lynx!"

Q: Where do baby elephants come from?

A: Huge storks.

Q: What kind of money did the baby wallaby have?

A: Pocket change.

Q: What's a bear's favorite rhythm instrument?

A: A tam-bear-ine.

Q: Where do baby elephants sleep?

A: In trunkbeds.

Q: Which cats were expelled from school because they had stolen the answers to the final exam?

A: The cheat-ahs.

Q: What did the baby wombat eat?

A: Pocket sandwiches.

Q: What looks like a large rat (like a bandicoot), with a long pointed nose (like a bandicoot) but is not a bandicoot?

A: A picture of a bandicoot.

Q: How does the king of beasts prefer to catch his dinner?

A: By lion in wait.

Q: How do tortoises keep warm?

A: They wear turtleneck sweaters.

Q: What are monkeys' favorite flowers?

A: Chimp pansies.

Q: When should you put an elephant in your sister's bed?

A: When you can't find a frog.

Q: What would you use to give a hippopotamus a flu shot?

A: A hippo-dermic needle.

Q: Why did a fast-food chain open a restaurant for primates?

A: They were hoping for a lot of monkey business.

Q: Why would pandas have been good actors in silent movies?

A: They excel at panda-mime.

Q: Why did the teacher put the deer in the corner?

A: He was moose-behaving.

Q: Which primate is able to fly?

A: The hot air baboon.

Q: When the fox family was dining on shore birds, what did the mother tell her hungry son?

A: "Wait for your tern."

Q: What's worse than having an elephant in bed with you?

A: Having two elephants.

Q: What time is it when a kangaroo jumps on your sofa?

A: Time to buy a new sofa.

Q: Why aren't there any elephants in outer space?

A: Because they take up too much inner space.

Q: What is the koala's favorite musical instrument?

A: The ukelele-lyptus.

Q: What food does a bear grill with his hot dogs?

A: Ham-bear-gers.

Q: What is the world's biggest pain in the neck?

A: A giraffe with a sore throat.

Q: What do bears spread on their toast?

A: Black-bear-ry jam.

Q: What kind of voice does Papa Bear have?

A: Bear-i-tone.

Q: Why are gnus afraid of catching colds?

A: They're worried they might develop gnu-monia.

Q: What's gray, has big ears and four legs, and weighs five pounds?

A: A very skinny elephant.

Q: What's a bear's favorite soda?

A: Root bear.

Q: What is as big as an elephant but weighs absolutely nothing?

A: An elephant's shadow.

Q: Can an elephant jump higher than a house?

A: Yes, houses can't jump at all.

Q: What green vegetable do bears like in their salads?

A: Cucum-bear.

Q: What is the meanest marsupial?

A: The Tasmanian devil.

Q: Do gorillas like orange juice?

A: No. They only like apefruit juice.

Q: Do oxen wear sneakers?

A: No. Only oxfords.

Q: What happened when the elephant tried to fix her neighbor's roof?

A: She brought down the house.

Q: What famous bear was born in a log cabin and became president of the United States?

A: A-bear-ham Lincoln.

Q: What do you call a bear fib?

A: A bear-faced lie.

Q: How does an elephant make a bedroll?

A: He pushes it downhill.

Q: Do grizzlies ever wear caps?

A: No. They always go bear-headed.

Q: Why was the bear's face red?

A: Because he was em-bear-assed.

Q: Why did the elephant eat under the lamppost?

A: She wanted a light lunch.

Q: What do primate youngsters love to play on in the schoolyard?

A: The monkey bars.

Q: What farm equipment does Farmer Bear use to carry rocks?

A: Wheel-bear-row.

Q: What happened to the elephant that swallowed his spoon?

A: He couldn't stir.

Q: What item that most tourists carry was invented by a bear?

A: The Kodiak camera.

Q: What's a bear's favorite kind of dancing?

A: Bear-eak dancing.

Q: What animal eats eucalyptus leaves and has a trunk?

A: A koala on vacation.

Q: Why wouldn't the ant rent his attic to an elephant?

A: He was afraid the elephant would put his foot down.

Q: What do you have when grizzlies fall into a vat of glue?

A: Gummy bears.

Q: What time is it when an elephant jumps rope?

A: Time to call for street repairs.

Q: Why did the elephant cross the road?

A: To prove she wasn't a chicken.

Q: What's the name of a famous World War II bear?

A: The Red Bear-on.

Q: Why is it hard to understand what turkeys say?

A: All they speak is gobbledygook.

Q: How can you tell if there's an elephant in your kitchen?

A: Look for footprints in the peanut butter.

Q: What ferocious fish did the bears see when they were snorkling?

A: A bear-racuda.

Q: How can you tell if your cook is an elephant?

A: He'll flatten the oatmeal cookies with his feet.

Q: At what events do bears grill hot dogs?

A: Bear-beques.

Q: How can you tell if there's an elephant in your milk shake?

A: It's really hard to suck anything up the straw.

Q: Why did the koala's dinner walk away?

A: Because eucalyptus leaves.

Q: In what Olympic event do elephants always take first place?

A: Herd-les.

Q: How does a bear wade through a creek?

A: Bear-foot.

Q: What happened to the elephant who slid into third base?

A: Nothing much happened to the elephant, but it was rough on the base.

Q: What famous statue welcomes bear immigrants to the United States?

A: The Statue of Li-bear-ty.

Q: What do you get when you cross an elephant with peanut butter?

A: An elephant that sticks to the roof of your mouth.

Q: What's a bear's favorite old-fashioned dessert?

A: Blue-bear-ry cobbler.

Q: Where did the bears go to snorkle?

A: The Great Bear-rier Reef.

Q: What does a bear eat when he's in Mexico?

A: Bear-ritos.

Q: What do you get when you cross a sheep, a hummingbird, and a beetle?

A: A baa humbug.

Q: Where do chimpanzees get most of their news?

A: They hear it through the apevine.

Q: How can you tell if an elephant is reading over your shoulder?

A: You can smell the peanuts on his breath.

Q: When will an elephant use your shower?

A: After a hot day of stampeding.

Q: What did the bear ride in when she went over Niagara Falls?

A: A bear-rel.

Q: What did the bear's friends say to him after he had blown out the candles on his cake?

A: Happy Bear-thday!

Q: How did Baby Bear feel when Mother Bear left on a trip?

A: Un-bear-ably sad.

Q: What is a gorilla's favorite dessert?

A: Chocolate chimp cookies.

Q: What do bears eat for breakfast?

A: Bear-an (bran) flakes.

Q: What do you do with a blue elephant?

A: Cheer her up.

This book is available in two editions:
Library binding by Carolrhoda Books, Inc.,
 a division of Lerner Publishing Group
Soft cover by First Avenue Editions,
 an imprint of Lerner Publishing Group
241 First Avenue North
Minneapolis, MN 55401 U.S.A.

Website address: www.carolrhodabooks.com

Library of Congress Cataloging-in-Publication Data

 Grin and bear it : zoo jokes to make you roar / by Sharon Friedman . . . [et al.] ;
pictures by Brian Gable.
   p.   cm. — (Make me laugh!)
   Summary: Presents a variety of jokes about animals.
   ISBN: 1–57505–660–7 (lib. bdg. : alk. paper)
   ISBN: 1–57505–741–7 (pbk. : alk. paper)
   1. Animals—Juvenile humor. 2. Zoos—Juvenile humor. 3. Wit and humor,
Juvenile. [1. Animals—Humor. 2. Jokes.] I. Friedman, Sharon, 1948– II. Gable,
Brian, 1949– ill. III. Series.
PN6231.A5G75 2005
818'.60208—dc22   2003019244

Manufactured in the United States of America
1 2 3 4 5 6 – DP – 10 09 08 07 06 05